CALUMET CITY PUBLIC LIBRARY

3 1613 00497 7969

P9-CBA-772

J
970.004
HAR
UTE

Pub. 20.00 4/16

SPOTLIGHT ON NATIVE AMERICANS

UTE

Lorraine Harrison

CALUMET CITY PUBLIC LIBRARY

New York

Published in 2016 by The Rosen Publishing Group, Inc.
29 East 21st Street, New York, NY 10010

Copyright © 2016 by The Rosen Publishing Group, Inc.

All rights reserved. No part of this book may be reproduced in any form without permission in writing from the publisher, except by a reviewer.

First Edition

Editor: Katie Kawa
Book Design: Samantha DeMartin
Material reviewed by: Donald A. Grinde, Jr., Professor of Transnational/American Studies at the State University of New York at Buffalo.

Photo Credits: Cover, pp. 5, 29 David W. Hamilton/The Image Bank/Getty Images;
p. 7 Don Fink/Shutterstock.com; p. 9 Danita Delimont/Gallo Images/Getty Images;
pp. 11, 17 courtesy of the Library of Congress; pp. 12–13 John Hoffman/
Shutterstock.com; p. 15 Evans/Hulton Archive/Getty Images; p. 19 George Frey/AFP/Getty Images; p. 21 Michael Buckner/Getty Images Entertainment/Getty Images;
p. 22 Ethan Miller/Getty Images Sport/Getty Images; pp. 24–25 DEA/L.Romano/
De Agostini/Getty Images; p. 27 Craig F. Walker/Denver Post/Getty Images.

Library of Congress Cataloging-in-Publication Data

Harrison, Lorraine, 1959- author.
 Ute / Lorraine Harrison.
    pages cm. — (Spotlight on Native Americans)
 Includes index.
 ISBN 978-1-5081-4129-7 (pbk.)
 ISBN 978-1-5081-4131-0 (6 pack)
 ISBN 978-1-5081-4133-4 (library binding)
 1. Ute Indians—Juvenile literature. I. Title.
 E99.U8H37 2016
 979.004'974576—dc23
                        2015031302

Manufactured in the United States of America

CPSIA Compliance Information: Batch #BW16PK: For Further Information contact Rosen Publishing, New York, New York at
1-800-237-9932

CONTENTS

PEOPLE OF THE WEST

CHAPTER 1

As Native Americans moved freely throughout North America before European settlers arrived, different groups began to settle in different areas of the continent. The land they settled on affected every aspect of their life—from the food they ate to the religious ceremonies they performed.

One large group of Native Americans—the Utes—settled in the western United States, with most of its population in what's now Utah and Colorado. The state of Utah is named after the Ute people.

Today, the Ute people still live mainly in Utah and Colorado. They're divided into three groups, or tribes. The Northern Ute Tribe, which is sometimes called the Ute Tribe, lives mainly on a **reservation** in northeastern Utah. The Southern Ute Tribe lives on a reservation in southwestern Colorado. A third and smaller group called the Ute Mountain Ute Tribe lives on a reservation in southwestern Colorado, southeastern Utah, and northern New Mexico.

Utes continue to honor the history of their people. Preserving their **culture** is very important to this proud group of Native Americans.

UTE HOMELANDS

CHAPTER 2

Utah and Colorado are the main homelands of the Ute people. However, the Ute people also called many other areas home before the arrival of white settlers. These areas included parts of present-day Wyoming, Nevada, New Mexico, and Arizona.

The Ute people traveled in family bands. All the bands were connected through a common language, which was part of the Numic language family. Other Native American groups who spoke languages belonging to this family included the Paiute and Shoshone peoples. Important religious events throughout the year brought these bands of Utes together.

From the Ute people's religious beliefs came their creation story, or the story of how they came to exist on Earth. According to Ute tradition, the Creator—also called Sinauf or Sinawav—gave Coyote a bag supposedly filled with sticks. When Coyote looked inside, he saw people instead. The people began to leave through a hole in the bag and spread out all over Earth. However, a small number were left behind, and they were placed in the sacred Ute homelands. These people were the first Utes.

Ute Canyon in Colorado, shown here, got its name from the Native Americans who called this area home long before European settlers arrived.

HUNTING AND GATHERING
CHAPTER 3

From their earliest days, the Utes believed in living in harmony with the land around them. When they hunted, they used every part of the animal, so nothing went to waste. Common animals hunted by the Utes included elk and other kinds of deer, as well as smaller animals such as rabbits and birds.

The Ute people also gathered wild plants. By observing the natural world around them, they learned a lot about which plants were safe to eat and which were the best for making medicines. Plants they gathered for food included wild onions and berries. Some Ute bands also planted crops, including corn and beans. However, they were mostly dependent on hunting and gathering instead of farming. In order to have enough to eat, they would walk across large areas looking for food. The Utes soon learned they couldn't come back to the same areas too frequently, because the **environment** needed time to recover from their hunting and gathering.

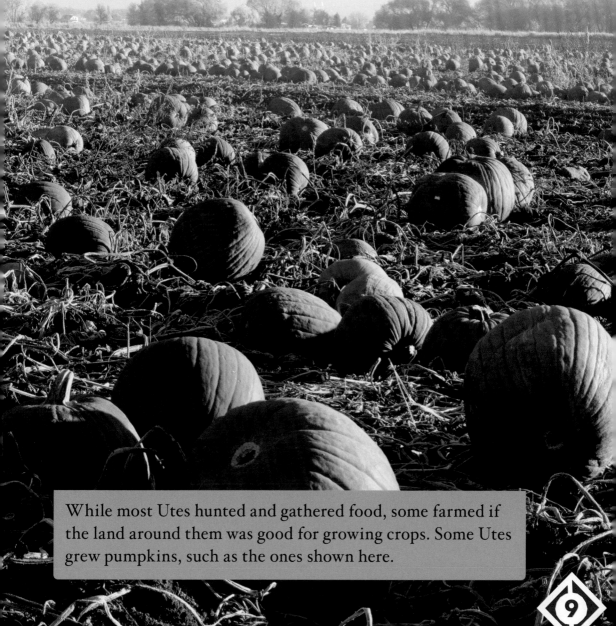

Early Utes made tools out of stone and wood to use when hunting and preparing food. They also became known for weaving baskets. They even found a way to seal the baskets they made to allow the baskets to hold water.

While most Utes hunted and gathered food, some farmed if the land around them was good for growing crops. Some Utes grew pumpkins, such as the ones shown here.

THE SPANISH ARRIVE

CHAPTER 4

The first Europeans to arrive in Ute territory were Spanish explorers. By the 1600s, the Spanish had entered Ute lands, forever changing the Ute people's way of life.

One of the biggest changes brought about by interaction with the Spanish was the introduction of horses into Ute culture. Horses allowed Ute hunters to move more quickly than ever before. This helped them hunt even larger animals, such as bison. As Ute hunters' skills at riding developed, bison became one of the most important sources of food for them.

The Utes were one of the first groups of Native Americans to acquire horses. This gave them an advantage over other communities. The Utes used their skills on horseback to **raid** neighboring communities, including the Apaches and Pueblos. The Ute people were known as brave fighters, and even women and children defended themselves and their land.

As contact and trade with the Spanish increased, the Utes were exposed to deadly diseases carried by the European settlers. **Smallpox** was one such disease that killed a large number of Utes because they had never been exposed to this disease before. Some Europeans also captured Utes and made them slaves.

Horses allowed the Ute people to travel farther from their homes than ever before. They often traveled east of their homelands as they hunted bison on horseback.

WHO OWNS THE LAND?

CHAPTER 5

The Utes and the European settlers had very different ideas of land ownership. The Utes, like most Native Americans, didn't believe anyone could own the land. They believed in living in harmony with it. However, the Europeans believed they owned the lands they settled.

This conflict over ideas of land ownership continued through the time of European colonization and into the

After gold was discovered at what's now called Pikes Peak in Colorado, even more white settlers flocked to lands that had once belonged to the Utes.

period of westward expansion for the United States. As white settlers from the eastern United States moved across the country, they crossed through Ute territory.

On December 30, 1849, the Utes signed a treaty with the United States in order to formally recognize the U.S. government and its power over them. This treaty also allowed U.S. settlers to continue to travel freely through Ute lands.

Pioneers saw the Ute homelands as profitable areas for settlement. These lands were rich in natural resources, including timber and water. There were also many wild animals for hunting and fur trapping. Even more settlers arrived in Ute territory when gold was discovered in Colorado in 1859. These settlers pushed Utes off their homelands and claimed the land belonged to them.

WAR IN UTAH
CHAPTER 6

As Utes in Colorado were losing their land to settlers looking for gold, Utes in Utah were fighting for their lands against the Mormons. Members of the Mormon religion traveled to Utah in the mid-1800s. They settled on Ute lands and claimed those lands for themselves.

From 1853 to 1854, the Utes and Mormon settlers fought what became known as the Walker War. The Utes led raids on Mormon settlements, but this war led to losses on both sides.

The peace that was established after the Walker War didn't last long. By 1865, a Ute leader named Black Hawk began leading more raids against the Mormons. These raids are sometimes known as the Black Hawk War. In 1868, Black Hawk and some of his followers **negotiated** a treaty with the settlers. Others continued raiding settlements until 1872. They weren't happy with Black Hawk because they felt he gave up too much land to the Mormons.

A Ute family is shown here on the Uintah and Ouray Indian Reservation.

Eventually, all the Northern Utes of Utah were relocated to a reservation established by the U.S. government in 1864. It was called the Uintah Reservation. It later **merged** with another reservation to form the Uintah and Ouray Indian Reservation.

ACCEPTING RESERVATION LIFE

CHAPTER 7

The Ouray Reservation, which joined with the Uintah Reservation in 1886, was named after a Ute leader named Chief Ouray. He was responsible for negotiating many treaties with the federal government on behalf of the Ute people. In 1868, he traveled to Washington, D.C., and was named the head chief of his people by the federal government.

That same year, a reservation was established for Southern Utes living in western Colorado. It was a large reservation that covered about a third of the state. However, the reservation's size was greatly decreased through the Brunot Agreement of 1873 after gold and silver were found on reservation lands.

Ouray's cooperation with the U.S. government during a difficult time in Ute history made him unpopular among some of his fellow Utes. In fact, some of them tried to kill him at different times throughout his life!

By the beginning of the twentieth century, most of the Southern Ute people were living on what's now called the Southern Ute Indian Reservation in Colorado. Reservation life wasn't easy for Utes. They were forced to learn English, and their traditional way of life began to disappear. Hunger and disease were common on reservations in the early 1900s.

Chief Ouray

CALUMET CITY PUBLIC LIBRARY

3 1613 00497 7909

TRADITIONAL DANCES
CHAPTER 8

When the Ute people were moved onto reservations, they were expected to give up their traditional religious beliefs and convert to Christianity. While many Utes converted, they also held on to some of the most sacred aspects of their traditional religion.

The most important religious ceremony for the Ute people is the Sun Dance, which happens every year in the middle of the summer. This ceremony is also known as "standing thirsty" because it involves the **participants** fasting, or going without food and water, for four days. During the Sun Dance, male Utes—who are called to participate through a spiritual vision—dance in order to obtain spiritual powers, which are also called "medicine powers." Participants in the Sun Dance are surrounded by their family for support.

During the spring, Utes participate in another religious ceremony known as the Bear Dance. It's one of the oldest ceremonies practiced by the Ute people. Today, it's known as a gathering of the Ute people that everyone can participate in. While only male Utes can take an active part in the Sun Dance, the entire Ute community can be a part of the Bear Dance.

Dances have always been an important part of traditional Ute religious beliefs. They serve as a way for the Utes to celebrate the changing of seasons, as well as other natural processes and experiences. These dances also serve as a way to bring Utes together.

UTES IN THE SPOTLIGHT

CHAPTER 9

Dance allows the Ute people to connect to their traditions, and it's also one way they share their culture with the world outside their reservations. Raoul Trujillo is a famous dancer and **choreographer** of both Ute and Apache **descent**. He was cofounder and the first choreographer of the American Indian Dance Theater. One of his dance pieces, which was called "The Shaman's Journey," was turned into a short film for public television. Trujillo is also an actor who's appeared in many films and television shows.

Joseph Rael, who also goes by a traditional name that means "beautiful painted arrow," is a famous Ute spiritual leader and writer. Rael has created new dances to help Utes and others around the world connect to their spirituality. He's turned his spiritual visions into books as well, including *Being and Vibration: Entering the New World*. He also wrote an **autobiography**, which is titled *House of Shattering Light: Life as an American Indian Mystic*. In addition, Rael is a painter whose works have been displayed in galleries throughout the western United States.

Raoul Trujillo is helping to bring Native American culture to the American public through his work in dance, television, and film.

NORTHERN UTES TODAY

CHAPTER 10

Life for Utes living on reservations today isn't always easy, but it's much better than it was in the early days of the reservation system. The Uintah and Ouray Indian Reservation is the second-largest reservation in the United States. It covers about 4.5 million acres (1.8 million ha) of land in northeastern Utah.

Successful businesses on the reservation provide jobs for those who live there. People raise cattle and mine for oil and natural gas on the reservation. They can also work at the reservation's supermarket, gas stations, and bowling alley, among other businesses. Water Systems is a reservation organization that provides water and **sewer** services to different communities.

Education is a major concern on the Uintah and Ouray Reservation. Tribal leaders are working to find ways to keep young people in school, because high school students are dropping out before finishing their education. Leaders encourage parents to be involved in their children's education. They also encourage elders to teach young people more about Ute history and culture than they learn in the classroom. This is a way for Northern Utes to continue to keep their traditional way of life alive.

The Uintah and Ouray Indian Reservation is near Salt Lake City, Utah. That's where the University of Utah is located. This school's sports teams are called the Utes. The Ute Tribe supports the school's use of their name as long as it's used respectfully.

UTE LIFE IN COLORADO

CHAPTER 11

Both the Ute Mountain Ute and the Southern Ute people of Colorado continue to find ways to preserve their culture in the modern world. For the Ute Mountain Utes, this is mainly achieved through Ute Mountain Tribal Park. Ute Mountain Utes give visitors tours of the park, explaining its landforms and how the park relates to Ute history. The Ute Mountain Utes also run a **casino** and a travel center. This tribe is the largest economic contributor in Montezuma County, Colorado.

The Southern Ute people operate many businesses and organizations both on and off their Colorado reservation. They run two radio stations through KSUT public radio. The Southern Ute people also run the Sky Ute Casino and Resort.

The Southern Ute Tribe is the largest employer in La Plata County, Colorado. It's always looking to create new jobs for its people in areas such as oil and gas production, **real estate**, and construction. The tribe does this through the Southern Ute Indian Tribe Growth Fund, which was created in 2000. This fund operates and manages the tribe's businesses.

Ute Mountain Tribal Park, shown here, is a place visitors can go to learn more about Native American history in Colorado.

A HELPING HAND

CHAPTER 12

While the Southern Ute Tribe runs many successful businesses, Southern Utes still face problems on the reservation. Proper care for children and the elderly, education, and job training are a few of the most important concerns being addressed by Southern Utes today. Alcohol and drug **abuse** are also problems facing some families on the Southern Ute Indian Reservation. There's a strong connection between unemployment rates and alcohol and drug abuse on the reservation.

In order to help Southern Utes deal with these areas of concern, Southern Ute Community Action Programs, Inc. (SUCAP) was created on October 10, 1966. Since then, it's grown into a large organization with the goal of creating better communities through providing helpful services to Southern Utes.

Young children and their families are assisted through the Southern Ute Head Start Program. The Early Head Start Program serves children, families, and pregnant women. The Ignacio Senior Center was established to help the elderly.

Also, job training programs are provided in 11 counties through SUCAP's The Training Advantage.

The difficult problems of alcohol and drug abuse on the reservation are handled by an organization called Peaceful Spirits. It provides treatment for people who are dependent on drugs or alcohol. It also provides information and support for their families. The Southern Ute Tribe is also working to create more jobs and improve educational opportunities for its people to help stop alcohol and drug abuse before they start.

Through SUCAP, the Southern Ute Tribe is doing what it can to help its people have every opportunity to succeed in life.

A STRONG IDENTITY

CHAPTER 13

People can travel to Ute reservations to learn more about Ute history and culture. Those interested in learning about the Ute Mountain Ute people can visit Ute Mountain Tribal Park and learn from Ute tour guides. People wanting to learn more about the Southern Ute people can visit the Southern Ute Cultural Center and Museum. This museum tells the story of the Southern Ute Tribe from its beginnings to the present.

Traditional Ute culture is still alive in the people who live on Ute reservations in Utah and Colorado. Through ceremonies such as the Sun Dance, Utes stay connected to each other and to their cultural roots.

Although the Utes have faced struggles throughout their history, they haven't given up their identity as a people. In fact, they're working harder than ever to combine that identity with life in the modern world. Through organizations such as the Southern Ute Tribe Indian Growth Fund and SUCAP, Utes are helping each other reach their full

potential. This has led to better job prospects, stronger economies, and healthier and happier members of all three Ute tribes.

Today's Utes are trying to build a better life for their children while helping those children understand the traditional ways of their people.

GLOSSARY

abuse: Improper or excessive use.

autobiography: A book that tells the story of a person's life that was written by the person it is about.

casino: A building used for gambling.

choreographer: A person who decides how a dancer or group of dancers should move during a performance.

culture: The beliefs and ways of life of a certain group of people.

descent: Referring to a person's ancestors.

environment: The natural world around us.

merge: To become joined.

negotiate: To discuss something formally in order to make an agreement.

participant: A person who is involved in an activity or event.

potential: An ability someone has that can be developed to help that person become successful.

raid: To carry out a surprise attack. Also, a surprise attack.

real estate: The business of selling land and buildings.

reservation: Land set aside by the government for a specific Native American group or groups to live on.

sewer: A system of pipes that carries water and waste away from buildings.

smallpox: A serious disease that causes a fever and a rash and is often deadly.

FOR MORE INFORMATION

BOOKS

Benoit, Peter, and Kevin Cunningham. *The Ute*. New York, NY: Children's Press, 2011.

Fadden, David Kanietakeron, and Barbara A. Gray-Kanatilosh. *Ute*. Edina, MN: ABDO Publishing, 2004.

Ryan, Marla Felkins, and Linda Schmittroth. *Ute*. San Diego, CA: Blackbirch Press, 2003.

WEBSITES

Due to the changing nature of Internet links, PowerKids Press has developed an online list of websites related to the subject of this book. This site is updated regularly. Please use this link to access the list: www.powerkidslinks.com/sona/ute

INDEX